DECEMBER 2021 EDITION

AN ANTHOLOGY OF ARTICLES

BRILLOPEDIA

ISBN 979-888569188-8

Contents

Contents

Preface

"Start writing, no matter what. The water does not flow until the faucet is turned on".

-Louis L'Amour

Hundreds of students and professors are contributing their work to Brillopedia, we are here to provide ample information about Law and Contemporary issues. Our aim is to provide a platform for today's generation to express their views and ideas on law and contemporary law.

CHAPTER ONE

HINDU MARRIAGE IS A CONTRACT OR SACRAMENT

Author: Arindam Pushkar, II Year of LL.B from Thakur Ramnarayan College of Law, Mumbai.

Arindam Pushkar

INTRODUCTION

India is the only country that adheres to religions in the context that Hindu religion has its own culture, conventions, cultures, and laws.

Marriage is considered a sacrament with solemn pledge under the Hindu Marriage Act of 1955, and it is not a contract that is only entered by the execution of a marriage. It is the mechanism by which our society will be carried forward. Everyone in society should understand what marriage seems to be. There is some debate in Society about whether marriage is a sacramental union or a contract. Marriage is defined as the establishment of a connection between a husband and a wife. Marriage, according to Hindu law, is a sacred bond and the last of 10 sacraments that can never be severed. It is also a bond that is formed from birth to birth. Even death, according to smritikars, cannot break this bond.

Similarly, there are 16 Samskaras, the most important of which is marriage (Vivah), which consists of seven steps and vows taken in front of a fire Sapta Padi. It's often regarded as a holy union, in addition to being sacred. The primary goal of marriage is to allow a woman and a man to fulfill their religious obligations. In addition to this, they must have progeny. A woman is considered half of her husband and so completes him, according to ancient literature. A man is considered incomplete without a woman. Is our Indian society prepared for this trend in light of the changing instances? Or does it require our conscious attention in way to sustain our society from circumstances? As a result, the purpose of this article was primarily to discuss both of these and try to reaching a conclusion.

WHY IS HINDU MARRIAGE A SACRAMENT?

A sacrament is a religious ceremony that is spiritual. Marriages between Hindus are recognized divine. There's no need for the girl's assent in ancient times. Where the fathers had to take decision about the boy without seeking her advice or consent. It is a religious bond between a man and a woman, but it is not a legally binding contract. It is also believed that Hindus have specific life missions, which are expressed by the 'purusharthas,' which include Dharma, Artha, Kama, and Moksha.

Marriage in Hinduism is regarded a religious sacrament since it is only valid when ritual and ceremonies are conducted.

The sacramental aspect of marriage has three elements.

1. It is an eternal connection that will be valid for all future lives.
2. It is regarded as a permanent connection since once tied, it cannot be dissolved.
3. Moreover, it is a sacred union in which religious ceremonies are required.

There is no requirement for either party's consent since that Hindu marriage is deemed sacred. Thus, the marriage is regarded lawful even if the person is of unsound mind or a minor.

SECTION 5 CONDITIONS FOR A HINDU MARRIAGE

A marriage may be solemnized between any two Hindus, if the following conditions are fulfilled, namely:—

I. neither party has a spouse living at the time of the marriage;

II. at the time of the marriage, neither party—

a) is incapable of giving a valid consent to it in consequence of unsoundness of mind; or

b) though capable of giving a valid consent, has been suffering from mental disorder of such a kind or to such an extent as to be unfit for marriage and the procreation of children; or

c) has been subject to recurrent attacks of insanity

III. which deals with the age of the parties specifically mentions that bride groom should be 21 years of age and bride should be 18 years of age , this are also the requisite of a contract.;

IV. the parties are not within the degrees of prohibited relationship unless the custom or usage governing each of them permits of a marriage between the two;

V. the parties are not sapindas of each other, unless the custom or usage governing each of them permits of a marriage between the two.

SECTION 7 OF HINDU MARRIAGE ACT PROVIDES

Ceremonies for a Hindu Marriage

(1) A Hindu marriage may be solemnized in accordance with the customary rites and ceremonies of either party thereto.

(2) Where such rites and ceremonies include the Saptapadi (that is, the taking of seven steps by the bridegroom and the bride jointly before the sacred fire), the marriage becomes complete and binding when the seventh step is taken

MARRIAGE AS A CONTRACT

The modern concept of marriage as a contract arose as a result of the industrial revolution and its lofty ideals of liberty and equality. The most significant contribution of the industrial revolution was the emergence of the concept that all human and social relations must be founded on the free violation of individuals. If human and social relations do not emerge from status and are based on the free violation of individuals. If human and social relationships do not emerge from status and are relationships that man has known, then marriage, too must be founded on the free violation of individuals. As a result, marriage came to be regarded as a legal contract.

Section 5 clause (ii) and (iii) of Hindu marriage Act content the pertinent provisions to deter mine Hindu marriage act as a contract.

CONCLUSION

According to Delhi High Court Marriage under the Hindu law is "sacrament" and "not a contract" which can be entered into by executing a deed.

Recently the Karnataka high court has observed that the Muslim marriage is a "contract with many shades of meaning, not a sacrament unlike a Hindu marriage" adding, that "such a marriage dissolved by divorce per se does not annihilate all the duties and obligations of parties by lock, stock and barrel".

As a result, in the greater part of Hindu marriages, a religious ceremony is observed. We can conclude that marriage contains contractual elements, but it is not solely contractual. Furthermore, it is recognized as a sacrament under the Hindu Marriage Act. As Hindu marriage is a holy and eternal union of two bodies, it is more of a sacrament.

Author's Bio

Mr. Arindam Pushkar is pursuing LL.B (2nd year) from Thakur Ramnarayan College of Law, Mumbai. He has graduated in BBA(Bachelor of Business Administration) from Sandip University, Nashik (Maharashtra). He has areas of interest in the fields of Constitutional Law, History, Ethics, Geography and Law.

CHAPTER TWO

DAMAGES

Author: K. Mihira Chakravarthy, I Year of B.A. L.L.B from Damodaram Sanjivayya National University (DSNLU).

K. Mihira Chakravarthy

Damages play an important role in awarding the compensation to the plaintiff after the tort is committed. It is one of the remedies which the injurer/ the plaintiff can avail. The damages are paid when there is an infringement of legal right and can go to the court i.e., Injuria Sine Damno. The awarded damages are unliquidated where the parties do not know each other or don't decide the amount before the commencement of the tort. The word damage and damages are two words which look alike though the meanings are different. Damage means the loss suffered by the wrongful act and damages is the compensation given to the injured by the injurer.

The court awards the damages in optimum way. It isn't neither over-compensated nor insufficient instead damages awarded are reasonable and sufficient. According to Article 226 of the Constitution, is a remedy in the public law. Whereas, the remedy lies in the ordinary law by a civil suit in law of torts and also the burden of proof lies on the plaintiff to claim the damages. An unascertained or unliquidated damage is the hallmark of tort actions.

There are types of damages awarded to the injurer like Nominal, Exemplary, Contemptuous, Aggravated, Compensatory damages.

There are three questions which the court enquires before awarding the damages:

1. Was the damage alleged caused by the defendant's wrongful act?
2. Was it remote?
3. What is the monetary compensation for the damage?

For a tort to be awarded damages, the Causation ('but for' test) which is to prove whether the wrong is caused any difference to the outcome of the result or not; Remoteness which include foreseeability which is the mitigation of the injury earlier itself and directness, that means the compensation for the amount of wrong they've committed.

The damages are the remedies which a claimant is awarded for the suffering because of the wrongdoer. The main objective in the civil litigation is to claim the damages.

Earlier, there used to be the direct redressal of 'an eye for an eye/ tooth for a tooth'. But later, it caused a lot of dissatisfaction and unjust in many situations and then raised the requirement of the monetary compensation for the civil wrong. Which was quite easy to determine in many cases especially in the torts.

The Roman law consisted the monetary compensation for the wrongs from very long and also this remedy was observed in the early development of the English law. Gradually, it became the primary remedy of the common law courts and the jury gave a lot of prominence in Anglo- American legal procedure. A body of legal doctrine decides the compensations that should be awarded to the particular wrongs.

Under tort law, the compensation is usually money value of losses or injury incurred by the plaintiff. The money value of any losses or injuries sustained as a "natural and proximate" result of the wrongful act. Since in the common law courts, a particular wrong can be challenged before the court only once, the damages are given to the plaintiff on basis of the injury suffered, injury which effects also the future.

For example: If the plaintiff has incurred a damage due to the negligence of the defendant, then the court after the examination of all the facts and evidences, decide the damages that are to be paid to plaintiff including the loss suffered, medical bills, future medical expenses that might occur due to the that wrong, loss of earning capacity etc., and also in some jurisdictions, the attorney fees are also taken from the defendant. If the defendant has conducted a wrongful act with a malicious intent, then the court might award the plaintiff with the punitive damages. In order to discourage the society's moral disapproval of the wrong done by the wrongdoer himself (i.e., the defendant).

TYPES OF DAMAGES

In a suit for damages in tort case, the court awards pecuniary compensation to the plaintiff for injury or damage caused to him by wrongful act of defendant. Various types of damages are:

- Nominal damages: When the plaintiff suffers the infringement of a legal right but no physical damages i.e., Injuria Sine Damno, then the nominal damages are awarded to him/ her.

In the case of Ashby v. White, the plaintiff was stopped from voting his representative but still the representative he wanted to vote has won. Here, even though the representative won and suffered no loss, his legal right was violated and the compensation was paid as damages.

- Contemptuous damages: The court has very low opinion on the plaintiff's claim, that even when the plaintiff has suffered loss, it was because of the earlier provocation by the plaintiff to defendant which caused injury. The court doesn't fully compensate the plaintiff.
- Compensatory damages: These damages are awarded to the plaintiff to get back to the situation before the commencement of the tort. These damages are easier when there are monetary losses as the same amount can be given to the plaintiff by the defendant.
- Aggravated damages: These damages are awarded by the courts, when the plaintiff goes through pain, agony and loss of self- esteem which have no monetary value. So, the additional damages are awarded other than

pecuniary damages.

In Ramesh Kumar Sharma v Smt. Akash Sharma, while filing divorce proceedings, the wife makes false allegations against her husband that he had illicit relations with his family member in the panchayat. She has made false allegations in the written statement. Taking that into consideration, the husband filed a case in Himachal Pradesh High Court and he was awarded Rs. 1.5 lacs as damages.

- Punitive/ Exemplary damages: These damages are awarded to the plaintiff when the tort conducted by the defendant is severely gross and to punish him from doing that and also others, the court decides to award Exemplary damages to the plaintiff.

According to Lord Devlin in the case of Rookes v. Barnard, he expressed those exemplary damages confuses the civil and criminal function of law and also held only in these 3 cases damages are granted

- Where the plaintiff has been aggrieved by oppressive, arbitrary or unconstitutional action by servants of the government, "though not when he is subjected to similar treatment by corporation's or private individuals."
- Where the defendant's conduct "has been calculated by him to make a profit for himself which may well exceed the compensation payable by him to the plaintiff Exemplary damages can properly be awarded whenever it is necessary to teach a wrongdoer that tort does not pay"
- Exemplary damages are exercised by the statute.

In the case of Bhim Singh v State of J&K, the exemplary damages were given to Bhim Singh as he was wrongfully detained while going to the Assembly session. Being the issue challenged in the Supreme Court, it ordered the Government of J&K to pay Rs 50,000 as damages for the wrong within 2 months.

- Prospective damages: These damages are claimed by the plaintiff due to the defendant's wrong which might cause future hindrances to the him and which has actually not occurred during the time of decision.

In Subhash Chander v Ram Singh, appellant Subhash was 7 years old and the respondent was the bus driver who caused accident to him. He couldn't stand without his surgical shoe and the disability wouldn't get him job in the future. The Motor Accidents Claims Tribunal, approved the compensation of Rs. 3000 under the heading of "Probable future loss by the reason of incapacity and diminished capacity of work". High Court of Delhi decided the damages to be Rs. 7,500.

MEASURE OF DAMAGES FOR PERSONAL INJURY

The personal injury's compensation is given under the following:

- There should be personal pain and suffering.
- Actual pecuniary loss resulting in any expenses reasonably incurred by plaintiff.
- Probability of loss of income by the plaintiff and future loss of work due to incapability.

A few case laws regarding the damages for personal injury:

- In the case of Laxminarayan v Sumitra Bai, defendant manipulated Sumitra Bai (plaintiff) saying that he would marry her if she had sexual relationship with him. After she became pregnant, he refused to marry her. The plaintiff was entitled to physical pain, indignity and was awarded with substantial damages under torts.
- In Union of India v. Savita Sharma, an 18year old girl who was travelling in a tempo had an accident with the military vehicle. She was severely injured and the court observed the agony she's gone through as she had to use an artificial leg to stand and that effects the future of hers like the marriage issue. She was awarded Rs. 10000 for medical expenses, Rs. 15000 for physical pain and agony, Rs. 12000 for permanent disablement, Rs. 6000 for expenses of Rs. 150 per year for replacing the artificial leg every year for 40 years which is the period of her life expectancy.

INTEREST ON DAMAGES

In addition to the damages, plaintiff is allowed 6% interest p.a. till the date of compensation. It is allowed in a few courts like Allahabad High Court and J&K High Court in a few cases.

DAMAGES IN CASE OF SHORTENING OF EXPECTATION OF LIFE

Injury caused by the defendant's negligence, when leads to the shortening of the life span of a person, the damages are offered to the plaintiff for the loss of a happy life.

- In the case of Flint v Lovell, the 69year old man who was injured in an accident was awarded for the damages. The trial Justice, Acton J. said that though he had a long, healthy and a very long happy life, the accident made him unhappy and inactive. Which is why court fixed £4000 and £400 were given as special damages.

Special damages: The wrongful act which injured the plaintiff might avail special damages, not in every occasion but only in a few special cases.

1. In the case of Benham v Gambling, a 2 ½year old baby died who lived in a happy and a healthy environment. This case was present before the House of Lords in 1942. The house issued 200 pounds as damages and set the following rules:

- The test to determine the compensation is based on the happy life but not the length of the life.
- Test of happy life is objective not subjective.
- Very moderate amount as damages is given.
- Economic and social position isn't taken into consideration of the deceased.

<u>DAMAGES UNDER NERVOUS & MENTAL SHOCK</u>

When a wrongful act or negligent act is occurred and the plaintiff suffers a psychological and mental hurt, the defendant/ injurer is held liable for that and is asked to pay the damages for the treatment of the plaintiff.

<u>DAMAGES UNDER THE FATAL ACCIDENTS ACT, 1855</u>

The damages for a wrongful act given to the dependents of the deceased. In case of Fatal Accidents, the dependents can claim under Indian Fatal Accidents Act, 1855. Section 1-A of the Act provides as under:

"Suit for compensation to the family of a person for loss occasioned to it by his death actionable wrong". – Whenever the death of a person shall be caused by wrongful act, neglect or default, and the act, neglect or default is such as would (if death had not ensured) have entitled the party injured to maintain an action and recover damages in respect thereof, the party who would have been liable if death had not ensued shall be liable to an action or suit for damages, notwithstanding the death of the person injured, and although the death shall have been caused under such circumstances as amount in law to felony or other crime.

The dependents who can claim compensation

The legal representatives under the Fatal Accidents Act are limited to children, parents, wife of the deceased person. Siblings, cousins, aunts and uncles can't avail the damages according to the act.

In Budha v Union of India, a suit was brought in by the brother of the deceased, mentioning himself the legal representative. The court has dismissed the case as the Act of Fatal Accidents don't mention brother as legal representative.

ASSESSMENT OF THE VALUE OF DEPENDENCY

The assessment of damages that is to be paid to the dependents in a proper way is determined by two different theories:

1. Interest Theory
2. Multiplier Theory

They are helpful to determine the quantum of compensation payable.

INTEREST THEORY

In this theory, the court determines the damages that is to be given to the dependent of the deceased. After the amount is decided, lumpsum amount is made to be paid, if deposited it should provide that much amount of interest which is equal to the sum that is determined by the court. For example: If M dies because of a tort committed by K, the dependent S would be left behind and he'd be having a monthly loss of Rs. 10,000. The Court will order the deposit of such amount from which the interest which is earned, is equal to Rs.10,000.

However, this theory has be declared inflexible principle in the case of,

Joki Ram v Smt. Naresh Kanta, the Full bench of Punjab and Haryana High court observed that the Interest theory is inflexible as the purchasing power decreases due to the run-away inflation.

MULTIPLIER THEORY

If any damage is likely to occur in the future because of the wrong committed by the defendant, the likely loss would be multiplied with the multiplier which indicates the number of years it might affect and the multiplication of amount is called as a Multiplier theory which is awarded by the court.

In the Municipal Corporation of Delhi v Subhagwanti, due to the negligence of the corporation, the clock tower at Chandni Chowk fell to the ground which fell on 3 members. The court awarded the dependents of the deceased members in a multiplier theory where the 3 members, income was Rs.40, Rs. 50 and Rs.150 and the amount was to be paid by the defendant to the dependents for 15 years with the amount of Rs. 7,200; Rs. 9,000; Rs. 27,000 respectively.

DAMAGES WHEN DECEASED IS NOT EARNING

For claiming the damages of a deceased person, the claimant should either be a legal claimant or supported by the deceased. In K. Narayana v P. Venugopala Reddiar, the plaintiff wanted to claim damages for the deceased wife as she died in a bus of the defendant due to his negligent driving. There was a point raised by the defendant that the wife had no income and the court then decided that to run the household, the wife who was a homemaker rendered Rs. 60 per month. Taking the life expectancy of the wife as 50 years, the court awarded Rs. 60,000 as damages to the husband to take care of himself and the children and the defendant to pay the amount for his negligence.

DAMAGES FOR THE LOSS OF CONSORTIUM

If there is a death of husband or a wife in a case, then the legal claimant can take the damages awarded for the injury i.e., death of them as they deprive the consortium of their life partner.

In the case of Narayana v P. Venugopala which was mentioned earlier, has taken the damages for his deceased wife, according to the Indian Fatal Accidents Act 1855.

In R.P. Sharma v State of Rajasthan, the petitioner's wife died because the hospital transfused B+ blood instead of O+. Due to the negligence of the hospital, the wife of petitioner became sick and died a painful death gradually. The court has awarded Rs. 3,04,000 as the damages for going through pain, agony and suffering and loss of company.

In the case of remarriage, M.P.S.R.T. Corp. v Sudhakar, after the death of her wife and the damages are given to the husband on the income of his first wife. After remarrying, the second wife had no income and the issue being challenged in the court, it was said that the second marriage wasn't the substitute of the first marriage and the loss still remains the same. The income of the second wife wasn't there, so the damages were still claimable by the husband of her first deceased wife. The Hight Court awarded Rs.

96,000 and on appeal the Supreme Court awarded Rs. 12,000 after assessing the loss on the account only as Rs.600 p.a. for 20years.

CONCLUSION

The damages are unliquidated in case of the torts as they don't fix the amount before the commencement of the tort. The types of situations during which the damages could be availed and also the claiming of damages when the person is deceased during a tortious act would be done by the legal claimants or the dependents of them.

Not only can a wife claim damages in case of husband's death due to the tort, even the husband can claim damages even if the wife doesn't have any income. The court takes the life expectancy of the deceased into consideration and the amount of income that the dependents might require for a period of time fixed by the court.

CHAPTER THREE

DOWNSIDE OF LINGUISTIC NATIONALISM IN INDIA

Author: Prashant shivaji Dound, I Year of B.A.,LL.B(Hons) from Maharashtra National Law University,Nagpur

Prashant shivaji Dound

Abstract

"Nationalism has a way of oppressing others"- Noam Chomsky

How can be the feeling of love and pride for one's language can be detrimental for the growth of people and their languages ? Linguistic nationalism is something which isn't new to India. It draws its history long back ago when India wasn't even an independent state. Traces of an evolved version of linguistic nationalism still exist today with different mechanism and fluid as compared what it consisted of in pre-independence stage. People might consider linguistic nationalism as in good light where people intent to protect and promote their own language but I aim to view it from not so popular view where I intent to study how the linguistic nationalism creates problems for the marginal minority speaker and to their language. Linguistic tussle is no new thing to India it could find its importance in politics and political representation too. Language getting align with politics is no wrong but it should be limited to certain level or else it creates problem for linguistic minorities .

Keywords: Detrimental, Growth, Linguistic, Minority, Nationalism, Politics, Representation.

Introduction/Primer

To understand the current tussle of linguistic nationalism which exist in India and the problem it creates for those people who are not loudly expressed in the society we would have to turn back some pages in history to understand the nuance of the scenario and how a term which shares its linkages to European soil came up on the Indian subcontinent.

Nationalism as a term draws its roots to the Europe where the concept of nationalism got developed, evolved and spread across the globe. India had imported modern nationalism from Europe. Though Indian nationalism doesn't share very much in common to the way Nationalistic feeling emerged in Europe and the way it emerged in India. Yet there existed a belief in the political corridor of our country in the 40s-50s (and it somewhat still exist today) to have a homogenous language throughout the country because that was apparently what European nationalism list as one of the essential to have successful nation-state(Though there exist many other reasons such as the desire to have own indigenous language in place of English which was believed to be as a symbol of colonial-era which existed in post-independent India. The formation of the nation-state in Europe, especially in Western Europe, was also based on building common linguistic homogeneity thus Nationalists believed to do so in India to foster the sense of collective belonging which was the prime reason for having homogeneity of language in the European nation-state. They believed doing so would strengthen the social fabric of the country but contradictorily to it, it caused many linguistic nationalistic outbursts in parts of India. Voices were raised against the blatant move of considering Hindi as the sole national language of the country after 1965. Protest erupted across the country especially in non-Hindi speaking states as the year 1965 came closer.

People were now taking much pride in their own linguistic culture and considered the formulation of Hindi as a national language as a dictatorial step, Though the subsequent government in power didn't allow it to happen due to ever-increasing linguistic nationalistic protest which might have further led to secession emotions among such state but the true achievement for these linguistic nationalist movements was the formulation of the 1956 State reorganisation commission's suggestion and formulation of state based on linguistic culture later on.

The Official Languages Act of 1963 retained the status of English as an official language of Public administration. Still, governments have tried to promote Hindi as a national language since it comes under its responsibility to promote Hindi in devnagri script across the state.

If we see the whole process in a sequence from a big picture view, one could easily conclude that these linguistic nationalistic movements saved the rich linguistic diversity of our country to date but when we zoom in on details then we realize this linguistic nationalistic movement and tussle between other big regionals languages might have sidelined the importance of certain marginal language which has very few takers in this movement of linguistic nationalism. This is where the researcher is going to research on.

Though the area of research on this topic can be very wide the author just wants to look at how these linguistic nationalistic feelings/movements might have disturbed or might have created problems for the marginal linguistic population in our country. Though there appears to be less literature on the same directly, the author also tries to take help from popular language statistics sources and regional news articles.

Rise of linguistic nationalism and the struggle for marginals

Linguistic nationalist movements in India have been regarded with great respect in society. Those leading such procession or protest were and are still considered as the true lover of their mother tongue .though they might be carrying good intention of promotion of their language or in against any forceful imposition of another alien language to them. But how can it cause trouble for the marginal (in sense with those people who speak a particular language which have less number of the speaker which might not put them up in the map of languages spoken in India or they might be scattered in the different territory of the jurisdiction where their language is not the majority language) is the question which must be of some great concern to us.

The number of languages facing the danger of getting wiped out is very large in India now. Devy, who documented 780 Indian languages while conducting the People's Linguistic Survey of India in 2010, also, shockingly, found that 600 of these languages were dying. Though various reasons might be playing their part here I believe one of the reasons might be excessive promotion and imposition of certain language by both state and central government in heat of linguistic nationalism.

Often in India promotion of one language has been done at the cost of another and it doesn't need to be proved in, one or other language has been always intended to replace in others e.g In the contention of making Hindi as the national language, other languages were discarded. This whole scenario has created repulsions in past and it still creates repulsion in the political corridor of Delhi.

Representation matters representation of elected members of parliament ensures that the voice of the linguistic minority (as compared to the Hindi)is heard. But how many languages in total do we have? There are a total of 121 languages that are considered mother tongues. Of these, 22 languages are included in the Eighth Schedule of the Indian Constitution.Are all of these 122 languages are represented in the Loksabha through their MPs? No, we can't infer that but people might be sure that 22 of the scheduled language might have representation in the parliament. What if I say there was a language that is among the scheduled languages which was spoken for the first time in the parliament in 2019? "'Santhali' reverberated in Rajya Sabha for the first time in 67 years since its inception when BJD MP Sarojini Hembram on Friday spoke in the language of the tribal community Santhals."

Santhali is one of those tribal languages which is showing a decline in growth. Take an example of Assam, before getting reorganised the bureaucracy of the Assam was dominated by the Bengali elites of Bengal who were having administration over local Assamese people and as the common middle-class aspiration of Assamese people grew on, the hatred towards Bengali people grew as they were considered as an outsider(of course the 1971 refugee crisis might have fuelled the hatred feelings) and this has raised into a tussle between Bengalis and Assamese in Assam.What

I want to highlight here is now that In between this tussle of languages there has been a decline of Santali in Assam. The number of Santali speakers fell from 2, 42,886 in 2001 to 2,13,139 in 2011 in the State.The same is the case with the Bodo in Assam.

One might also believe why is there even a need for a justifiable linguistic representation of language groups in parliament. Well, the answer is quite simple it's easier to raise the concern of the respective linguistic group at a national stage and what can be the best public national stage other than the floor of parliament but how it becomes difficult for such linguistic cultured people to even send their representation in the parliament? well the reason is that they aren't concentrated at one place. Santhali is the language which is spoken in more than 7 states.Though in a few states such as Chhattisgarh ,Odisha , Bengal you would get some takers of the language and supporters but in other states where this particular linguistic group has less numbers and hence doesn't provide any political parties with any political mileage, thus there concerns remain unheard and unrepresented. Well, one can always give credit to India's robust democratic freedom and system which didn't allow any radical imposition of a single language over such a diverse society.

We all know that linguistic diversity in north east is quite rich as compare to what one might observe in the Gangetic plains though the number of dialects of the same language can be varried but when it comes to an functional understandable language then it all boils down to Hindi . As many as nine languages have a significant number of speakers among the tribal people in Manipur, while in Uttar Pradesh only one language is widely spoken but when it comes to representation of language in the parliament about 90% of 80 seats of UP can be sure shot representing MPs belonging to the linguistic group of Hindi which is also spoken by 90% of the population of UP but when it comes to Manipur it sends 2 representatives to the loksabha assuming that 1 one of them might be from the dominant Manipuri language the rest 1 can't be represented by other language 8 prominent language groups . This example was only taken to create an image of what scenarios exist in our country as of now .What I fear is that if this linguistic nationalistic movements strike up again then who would be representing this and other fellow marginal languages which remain unheard in the power politics of the Linguistic nationalism .One might even argue that there is no need of such marginal languages to be represented at national level but it doesn't appears so easy in India's case. Each marginal language

/tribal language is connected with a specific tribe or group of people and if we create such circumstance where they have no way but the only way is to adapt to a new language, all together that means slowly shedding out old linkages and getting assimilated in the mainstream but this all together doesn't sound rightful in the context of article 29 of Indian constitution which lays down that It provides that "any section of the citizens residing in any part of India having a distinct language, script or culture of its own, shall have the right to conserve the same." Moreover, in the article 350(b) it says that a "Special Officer for Linguistic Minorities appointed by the President of India to investigate all matters related to safeguarding of that linguistic minorities in under Indian constitution"

Which sought of indirectly demands the state(government) to look into linguistic matters of minorities but again the vicious cycle reaches up here "where are the linguistic minorities representing in the government?" to look into the matter and take faster cognizance of matters.

That's how it becomes important for the representation of representatives in parliament who can raise their voice of concern towards the government and seek their attention. But since these linguistically different people are so less in numbers it becomes practically difficult for them to do so.

winning election, the only way to ensure representation?

Well, one can say that getting elected to parliament is not the only way one can become part of the government but one can always participate in civil services exam which fairly gives level ground for everyone but there comes another restriction or deterrence here in play that is the availability of quality resources and material in indigenous language for such linguistic minority people.There are still many states which still only provides limited option of language to pursue education, even it becomes difficult for a linguistic minority people to pursue primary education in their language. Take an example of NCERT books which are considered as primary source material for Civil services aspirants, it officially gets printed only in English, Hindi and Urdu. Though a translated version of the same might be available through private channel, publishers would also see his profit margin here and would try to limit and sale translated copies in popular languages other than these three. So it again leaves them with a gap of knowledge available in their indigenous.

Driving to the Hotspot: South India

South India is that part of India which has stood up first in driving up of the linguistic nationalistic feeling among the common people and made the others realise that we care for language much more than anything other and we won't welcome any other imposition of language even if it's also driven by another linguistic nationalistic feeling.

Kasargod's linguistic diversity

Now let's see another case that can be directly related to the tussle between linguistic nationalistic movements. This time we would move in south. It's the district of Kasargod, Kerala adjoining the southern part of Karnataka. The district as a whole has been dominated by Malayalam speakers (80%) and the notable linguistic minority here is Kannada and Tulu. Here Malayalam and Karnataka have their linguistic state and due to linguistic politics here the concerns of the Kannad people in Kasargod is often raised by Karnataka's politicians. Things take great turns here if it's related to language or any of the things related to the minority here for example There were rumours in Kasargod about just renaming of names of certain villages in Kasargod former C.M of Karnataka a wrote letter about his concern about the same to the current CM of Kerala to take his assurance which was given by so. "Kerala Chief Minister Pinarayi Vijayan on Tuesday informed former Karnataka Chief Minister Siddaramaiah that no decision has been taken to change the name of any village in the Kasaragod district of Kerala."When letters are just exchanged between CMs you can understand the intensity of emotions which are among people here and politics related to it but linguistic Nationalistic back in Kerala might not even like this attempt of interference from their counterparts in Karnataka they might also want to promote their language itself. This is quite obvious from the steps which were taken by the Kerala government in the Kasargod. The government has again begun its habit of posting Malayalam mother tongue teachers to Kannada medium schools located in the border areas of Karnataka and Kerala.

These steps are quite evident not only in Kerala but also throughout the country where such scenarios exist. Though on paper the Government very proudly says that "We are protecting linguistic minority community" it's hard to see it on the ground.

In such scenarios, it's often seen that such people are often considered as outsiders by the government bureaucratic babus(officers) and they often don't consider themselves duty-bound to serve them because those holding these positions are always from the linguistic dominant community as exams of these particular post is often conducted in two to few languages only.

For e.g In Kerala, The Kerala Administration exam is conducted in English and Malayalam as of now. But authority leaders have promised to include Kannada and Tamil in future. One thing which must be seen here is that there was no mention of the inclusion in Tulu in future.

Tulu is a language that is spoken in southwestern Karnataka and northern Kerala

Even though Tulu is considered one of the Pancha Dravida Bhashas (the five prominent languages of South India), it never found a place in the 8th Schedule of the Constitution as an official language. what's more concerning about this language is its very own nature which makes it a kind of oral language where you won't find much of the written literature in Tulu moreover the literature you would find is written in Kannada script which would harm its distinct identity as compare to Kannada . As feared according to the Atlas of the World's Languages in Danger, published by U.N.E.S.C.O, Tulu is now considered a vulnerable language. But how come is linguistic nationalism related to here? Karnataka as a state was reorganised as a kannad linguistic state and the politics of the state had been revolving around the languages in the past. Among the four southern states, it has the least proportion of its population (66%) reporting Kannada as the mother tongue, compared with more than 85% in Tamil Nadu and (undivided) Andhra Pradesh, and 97% in Kerala, reported this paper, using 1991 data, from the Institute of Social and Economic Change This makes it quite clear why Karnataka despite being formed under the banner of linguistic reorganisation process carries insecurity with itself about its language. Hence the state wants to promote it at all possible levels. One such incident indicating the sensitivity of the state concerning language was the blackening of the nammametro Bengaluru signboards which were written in Hindi.

The issue of Belgaum (Belgavi) is also a similar case of linguistic nationalistic tussle between Marathi speaking and kannada speaking majority.Since the district of Belgaum comes under the jurisdiction of Karnataka it has tried to promote the kannad language in there. Various political pressure groups from both side often blacken the placard or banners in Belgaum if found written in other language than the one which they are promoting. Marathi people here are at a disadvantage when it comes to participating in the KPSC(Karnataka Public service commission)

Exams. In the Belagavi district, Marathis account for 38% population. The Karnataka government has made knowledge of Kannada compulsory for government jobs. But there is hardly any Kannada school in the district The linguistic tussle has moreover taken a violent turn where you would find up news articles over physical manhandling of people and discrimination in mainstream media. Though there might be other political intentions playing their part here one can't deny the involvement of linguistic nationalist sentiments here. The Marathi people here want to join Maharashtra because they feel their language would provide them with a greater sense of belongingness with Maharashtra. Of course, other reasons always do exist.

More recently the state government of Karnataka had issued two orders mandating the inclusion of Karnataka in degree college courses which was eventually dragged into court where the court orally observed that the state can't impose Kannada upon students coming outside from the state.

These orders were certainly unwanted for a state which is emerging as one of the educational hubs of India still the state of Karnataka like few others also is struck by the wave of linguistic nationalistic feel where the state appears to be more insecure with regarding its language and in wake of this, the state is pursuing steps which might promote its language but finally at what cost? The cost of other fellow languages.

CONCLUSION

The linguistic nationalist movement which appears to have ended is not ended but still exist in its own form of new fractions. Though the aim of this fractions is different from that of past movements where the conservation of linguistic culture and to stop the imposition of Hindi was the primary aim (in most of the cases as against to Hindi nationalistic movement where the aim was more of imposition of language throughout the state) It has more turn into a promotion of languages with linguistic nationalist backing where they appear to be more sensitive and tries to protect the interest of their linguistic cultured people where their number might be lacking. But not all languages and people have the same linguistic nationalist backing and those who don't have such as santhali is facing a decline in regions where it's not so dominant.

States reorganised on the basis of languages aren't accepting or aren't open-minded in recognising linguistic minority of their state neither they appear to be dedicated towards preservation of such linguistic minority and somewhat these intentions appear to be driven by linguistic nationalist feelings which appear to be outclassing the feeling of inclusive diverse culture which used to be at first place the face value of such linguistic nationalism culture which first started in India in the past

Author's Bio

Prashant Shivaji Dound was born in Bharatpur of Rajasthan and have lived in various numerous parts of India namely Rajasthan , Madhya Pradesh , Uttar Pradesh and Maharashtra which has helped him in getting first hand experience of different culture and languages. He currently resides in Maharashtra and has completed his schooling from Kendriya vidyalaya & Army Public School .He is pursuing his graduation in B.A-L.LB(Hons) from eminent National law University ,Nagpur.

CHAPTER FOUR

HUMAN TRAFFICKING: A CURSE TO THE SOCIETY

Author: Anuja Saklani, V year of B.A.,LL.B. from Delhi Metropolitan Education, Guru Gobind Singh Indraprastha University.

Anuja Saklani

INTRODUCTION

As said by Edmund Burke "Slavery is a weed that grows on every soil."

Human trafficking is one of the most horrific crimes that exist in our society. Not only in our society, but throughout the whole globe this phenomenon is growing rapidly. Human trafficking which is also known as "trafficking of human beings" as a crime affects people irrespective of their caste, creed, religion and gender. Human trafficking is deeply rooted in our system. So here are few definitions on human trafficking given by different organizations/ websites.

According to United Nations Protocol to Prevent, Suppress and Punish Trafficking in Persons: "The recruitment, transportation, transfer, harboring or receipt of persons, by means of the threat or use of force or other forms of coercion, of abduction, of fraud, of deception, of the abuse of power or of a position of vulnerability or of the giving or receiving of payments or benefits to achieve the consent of a person having control over another person, for the purpose of exploitation."

According to Huff post "Human trafficking is a form of modern-day slavery. It's the exploitation of people and involves the use of force, fraud or coercion to obtain some type of labor or commercial sex act."

According to the Oxford American Dictionary "the crime of transporting or controlling people and forcing them to work in the sex trade or other forms of forced labor."

Human trafficking is a serious threat which prevails in the society that violates the rights of the human beings.

FORMS OF HUMAN TRAFFICKING

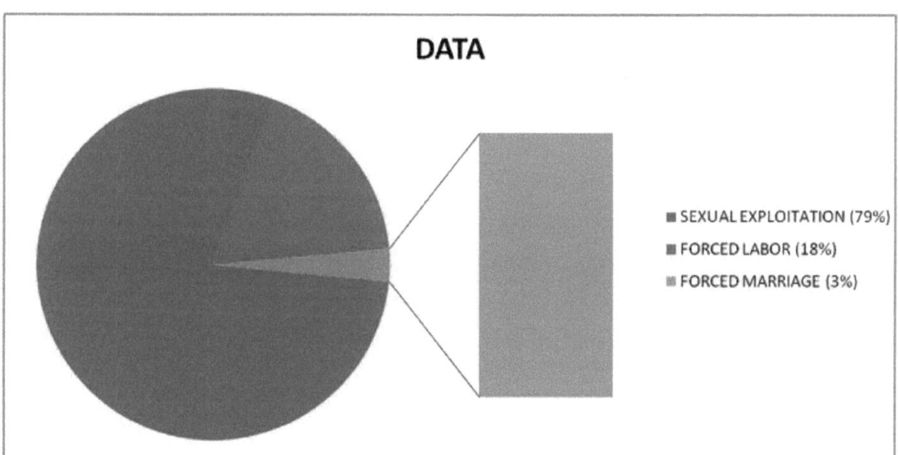

According to Global Report on Trafficking in Persons' by the United Nations Office on Drugs and Crime (UNODC), the most common form of human trafficking is sexual exploitation (79%). Generally the women and the girls are the sufferers of sexual exploitation. The second most form of human trafficking is forced labor (18%). Men and boys are generally the victims of forced labor.

Forced marriage is also a form of human trafficking where a woman is sent abroad, forced into the marriage and then frequently forced to engage in cohabitation. All over the world, out of all the trafficking victims 20% are children.

REGIONS WHERE HUMAN TRAFFICKING IS ON RISE

- Areas such as Andhra Pradesh, Madhya Pradesh, Rajasthan, Orissa, Uttar Pradesh, Bihar Karnataka and West Bengal are such places where human trafficking is on rise.
- Nationwide, Assam holds the highest position of child trafficking cases.
- Bangladesh secures the first position with the highest rate of human trafficking in the world.
- Poor and poverty stricken areas of the society, of the world where awareness, education and employment possibilities are very sparse.

EFFECTS OF HUMAN TRAFFICKING

There are several serious effects of human trafficking which directly affect the victims which are as follows:

1. MENTAL SUFFERING: The mental suffering, the mental agony through which a victim of human trafficking goes is something which cannot be explained. The mental stress that is there on their mind is devastating and due to which they may experience memory loss, agitation, uneasiness, misery and several other kinds of mental agony.

2. PHYSICAL SUFFERING: Generally the victims of sexual exploitation, which is a form of human trafficking experience physical suffering. Such victims are afraid of establishing new relations with people. They may be beaten up burned and raped by the trader and the customers. There is also a fear of sexually transmitted diseases like HIV and AIDS. Lack of proper medical facilities even worsens the situation.

3. SOCIAL EXCLUSION: Victims of human trafficking often face social exclusion. They are secluded from their friends circle, social circle etc.

STEPS TAKEN BY THE UNITED NATIONS TO COMBAT THIS PRACTICE

These include –

1. UN Office on Drugs and Crime (UNODC) aided many NGOs in the fight against human trafficking.
2. The United Nations Global Initiative to Fight Human Trafficking (UNGIHT) was formulated to promote the global fight against human trafficking.
3. United Nations Voluntary Trust Fund for Victims of Trafficking in Persons, 2010; which is there to provide humanitarian, legal and financial aid to victims of human trafficking.

HUMAN TRAFFICKING AND INDIA

Human trafficking is rapidly growing in many parts of India. Regions like Bihar, Rajasthan, Uttar Pradesh, Andhra Pradesh, Madhya Pradesh, West Bengal and Assam are such places where this heinous crime is on rise. Delhi is becoming the new hotspot for human trafficking. Here girls are being sold for the purpose of prostitution, sexual exploitation and to work as a bonded labor. The situation is quite worse now. As per the reports of Indian Government human trafficking rose by 20% in 2016 against the previous year. According to National Crime Records Bureau (NCRB) there were 8,132 human trafficking cases last year against 6,877 in 2015, with highest number of cases reported in the state of West Bengal followed by Rajasthan in the West.

STEPS TAKEN BY THE GOVERNMENT OF INDIA

- The Indian Government enacted "The Immoral Traffic (Prevention) Act, 1956 (ITPA) "which is the primary legislation for prevention of trafficking for commercial sexual exploitation.
- Anti- trafficking Nodal Cell was also established by the Ministry of Home Affairs.
- The Government of India enacted Protection of Children from Sexual offences (POCSO) Act, 2012, which is a special law to protect children from sexual abuse and exploitation.
- The Ministry of Women and Child Development made first ever anti-human trafficking law to fight back against human trafficking.
- Funds for rehabilitation and other issues of the victims of human trafficking are provided by the government.
- For effectively tackling the serious issue like human trafficking, the Ministry of Home Affairs appointed several advisories.

- India and Bangladesh signed a MOU for Prevention of Human Trafficking in Women and Children.
- Sections 366(A) and 372 of the Indian Penal Code (IPC) prohibit kidnapping and selling minors into prostitution.
- Programme such as "Ujjawala" is also implemented by the Ministry of Women and Child Development which is concerned with rescue, reformation of victims.
- Article 23, of the Constitution prohibits "Traffic in human beings and other similar forms of it"
- The Government has even launched a website known as "Lost and Found" or "Khoya Paya" to help the families to trace the children who have been missing since ages and has been abducted for sexual exploitation or forced labor.

CONCLUSION

Even though several attempts and efforts have been taken by the Government of India and worldwide too but still this menace is prevailing in the society. In order to remove this menace from the society stringent rules and laws should be made. Making of rules and laws will not help until and unless they are implemented strongly. So it is the implementation process that is important. Different and innovative programmes should be held to aware people about human trafficking. It's high time that we stand against this menace, before it's too late.

Author's Bio

My name is Anuja Saklani and I am a 5th year student pursuing BA.LLB from IP University. I have been writing since I was in my 1st year of the graduation. I have an immense passion for writing on different socio- legal topics that exist in our society. My paper titled "Human Trafficking: A Curse to the Society" got such a great platform like Brillopedia. Thank you Brillopedia.

CHAPTER FIVE

A REVIEW ON THE NEW UAE LABOUR CODES: WHAT TO EXPECT AND WHAT STILL NEEDS A CHANGE

Author: Srabasti Bhattacharyya, IV year of B.A.,LL.B(Hons.) from Amity University, Kolkata

Co-author: Sreeparna Sekhar Bhattacharjee, IV year of B.A.,LL.B(Hons.) from Amity University, Kolkata

On issuance of his highness, Sheikh Khalifa bin Zayed Al Nahyan, the Federal Law No.33 of 2021, the newly amended law of the United Arab Emirates will come into effect from the 22nd of February 2022 thus repealing the current labour laws which have been there since 1980.

The main area of focus shall be the private sectors in the UAE which shall encircle free zones excluding the Dubai International Financial Centre along with the Abu Dhabi Global Market, thus being able to implement their personal labour laws.

The government while declaring the labour law changes ensures that the new laws will protect the employer's and employees' rights to ensure more flexible working models for the post-Corona Virus workplace.

This new law has undergone significant amendments. These changes will only affect private-sector employees and companies, including free zones. The researchers have put together the most important modifications which have been enumerated as under:-

Anti-discrimination and anti-harassment protection

With the new amendments showing positive perks, UAE makes discrimination based on race, colour, sex, religion, national origin, or disability of an individual an offence. The employers, supervisors, and co-workers shall face severe repercussions if they sexually harass, bully, verbally or physically abuse an employee.

An employer shall not coerce or threaten an employee into performing work or providing services against their will. Employers should not dismiss or threaten to terminate, a female employee because she is pregnant or on maternity leave.

The employers who violate the New Labour Law may face fines ranging from AED 5,000 to AED 1,000,000 (not payable to affected employees).

Providing employees with a flexible working model

The new changes in part-time, temporary and flexible works aim to provide the UAE labour market with more flexibility.

Under Part-time work, employees can work for many employers for a set number of hours or days, either on-site or remotely, as specified in the respective contracts.

In Temporary employment, employment is based on the assigned project or a task basis. Contracts come to an end when the assigned work on each contract is completed. Under flexible work, Employees shall work on different days and times based on the working conditions and criteria under this scheme's contracts based on job conditions and requirements.

Employees can set their working hours in consultation with the employer. Furthermore, the New Law allows employees to work remotely from anywhere in the UAE, with the approval of their employer.

The abolition of long-term contracts

The option of endless employment contracts will not be valid after February 2, 2022. Limited (fixed-term) contracts will be required for federal government institutions and private businesses, which shall need renewal once or numerous times for a certain duration as agreed by both sides.

The existing system of unlimited contracts will be phased out over time. For the private sector, the new labour law, which was announced recently, replaced limitless contracts with limited contracts of no more than three years.

Changes in leaves

I. Annual leave: Full-time federal government and private-sector employees are entitled to a 30-day annual leave each year. Employees working for six months are permitted two paid days off for each month available in the year. Employees who choose temporary, part-time, or flexible work contracts will have their annual leave calculated following the new laws.

II. Maternity leave: In the private sector, maternity leave will last 60 days, with 45 days at full pay and an additional 15 days at half pay. For the first six months after conceiving, new mothers are entitled to one hour every day for breastfeeding once they return to work. Companies cannot terminate a worker for taking maternity leave. Employees‘ maternity-related "sick" leave has also been reduced from 100 to 45 days in a consecutive or intermittent manner.

III. Paternity leave: Men are entitled to a five-day paternity leave that can be either consecutively or over the first six months after the birth of their child. Employees are entitled to five days off for the death of a spouse and three days off for the death of an immediate family member as compassionate leave.

IV. Sick leave: Employees are entitled to at least 90 days of sick leave each year, with 15 days paid, 30 days at half pay, and the rest unpaid.

V. Study leaves: Employees enrolled in a UAE-accredited educational institution or university, whether inside or outside the country, are entitled to ten days off each year on account of study leave.

Employee termination during the probationary period

If an employee wants to relocate to another company in the UAE, he/she can terminate his/her contract during the probationary period by giving the employer at least one month's written notice.

In this scenario, the New UAE Labour Law stipulates that the new employer must reimburse the prior employer for any costs associated with the employee's recruitment.

If an employee chooses to leave the UAE during his/her probationary period, he/she must give at least 14 days written notice to terminate his/her employment. In such cases, where the employee returns to the UAE and secures a work visa from the Minister of Human Resources and Emiratisation (MOHRE) within three months of departure, the new company must reimburse the old employer for any recruitment expenditures expended.

End of service benefit

According to the new law, an employee who has worked for the company for one year or longer is entitled to an end-of-service gratuity when they leave. Those who work for up to five years will be entitled to a gratuity calculated based on 21 days of compensation for each year of service.

If an employee has worked for more than five years, the gratuity will grow to 30 days of income for a year's service. If the employee stays with the existing employer until the New Employment Law takes effect, the New Employment Law will apply to the respective employer.

Minimum Wages

Article 27 of the New Law will establish a minimum salary for the first time in the UAE. Following a request from the MOHRE, in conjunction with the necessary agencies, the UAE Cabinet will determine and announce the minimum salary amount.

Retention of Passports

The retention of an employee's passport is expressly forbidden by law.

Overtime

Overtime will be limited to 144 hours for every three weeks and computed based on the employee's basic income.

Recommendations for more reforms that needed more spotlight

After 1980, this is the first time where the labour laws are being extensively changed. But has this vast change in the laws have been able to meet international standards? the Human Rights Watch has taken a stand on the newly proposed laws and has also recommended a few changes which could have been given importance as well.

1. Right to form a trade union and collective bargaining

The International Labour Organisation (ILO) states that one of the fundamental rights is the freedom of association and effective acknowledgment of the right to collective bargaining. The UAE, being a member must go by and protect this right.

However, the new UAE labour law does not protect the same and has no provisions in its draft which have been able to recognize any workers' right to form and join a trade union or the right to collective bargaining. In the year, 2006, the UAE Labour Ministry had made it official that the law concerning the absence of the right to trade union would be considered but even the recent amendments have failed to take up this concern.

If this right is not given to the workers, then concerns relating to the workplace, the government and their own employers remain underground. This is a violation of their fundamental rights which the ILO Declares. It violates their opportunity to communicate their injustice to the appropriate authority.

2. Discrimination on the Basis of Sex

International laws strictly denounce discrimination in terms of employment. In the exercise of the right to work, to free choice of employment, and to equitable and suitable working conditions, there shall be no discrimination based on gender. The ILO, also recognizes that there should be no discrimination in terms of 'occupation'. Enshrined as a fundamental right of the workers, UAE has to include them in its laws and protect international standards.

The UAE has prohibited women from working at night, prevents women from working jobs that are hazardous (Article 30). Intending to protect its women, the UAE law bars women from having the freedom to choose their profession in a free manner.

The government must take steps to protect them and ensure safe working conditions for both men and women. It should instead let the person in an entirety decide whether to work in those circumstances or not.

The Human Rights Watch mentions that these prohibitions on women cannot be defended under the ambit of protection of women. The clear difference in sexes has affected the promotion of women in their areas of work.

Article 35 of the newly proposed laws scream discrimination as it demeans women under the control of their male counterparts, who can restrict women from all employment. There must be equality before the law and equal protection of the law irrespective of the gender a person identifies in. Thus, there rises a severe need to amend Articles 25-35.

3. Workers' strikes should be a right

International law protects the freedom to strike. The ICESCR supports "the right to strike," and the ILO Committee on Freedom of Association acknowledged the right to strike as an "essential aspect of trade union rights" in1952.

The UAE labour law needs an amendment to safeguard the workers right to strike particularly by creating clear processes for exercising this right, such as strike vote requirements and strike notification laws.

The proposed law violating workers' right to strike under Articles 155-166 requires that any group labour issues that cannot be handled amicably between the parties be brought to the Group Labor Disputes Conciliation Committee for binding settlement.

Unless the Committee's judgement is appealed to a court, whose judicial ruling becomes binding on the parties, the proposed law states that the Committee's decision is "final and enforceable." Such obligatory binding arbitration, according to the ILO Committee of Experts, violates international standards.

4. A Check on Child Labour

The Human Rights Watch has commented that there are internal oppositions that can create confusion as to the minimum age for children working. The provisions in the UAE law must be in accordance with the ILO Convention.

But that is not the case. A child is termed as a person of "thirteen years of age but below eighteen years of age". This could awaken confusion related to the age group which has been mentioned because children of that age group are not supposed to work.

CONCLUSION

However, there have been certain historical changes as well like the amendment of Article 15 where the employers to provide the workers with the expenses for the migrant workers in terms of travel, medical expenditure and other costs as and so required. On the other hand, Article 85 deals with employers' need to cover their employees' health care on arrival.

Workers are the pillars of our society. The laws are needed to be changed when it comes to the needs of the workers and their protection. The changes made were necessary for the workers' rights with an urge to protect their rights as well.

CHAPTER SIX

CHILD LABOUR- TACKLING THE PROBLEM

Author: Roshni Agarwal, II year of B.A.,LL.B.(Hons.) from Amity Law School Noida (ALSN)

Roshni Agarwal

Child labour and poverty are inevitably bound together, and if you continue to use the labour of children as the treatment for the social disease of poverty, you will have both poverty and child labour to the end of time.

What is Child Labour?

The International Labour Organisation (ILO) defines child labour as work that deprives children of their childhood, potential and dignity, and is harmful to their physical and mental development. It refers to the work that is mentally, physically, socially or morally dangerous and harmful to children, or work whose schedule interferes with their ability to attend regular school, or work that affects in any manner their ability to focus during school or experience a healthy childhood.

World Day Against Child Labour on 12 June

Child Labour- an ILO and UNICEF Report (Published on 10th June, 2021)

Cobalt is a mineral essential to the rechargeable lithium-ion batteries that powers smartphones, laptops and electric vehicles. The mobile phones which we enjoy contains this mineral cobalt which is extracted from mines by children. It is all mined by use of child labour or child slavery.

According to UNICEF, more than 40,000 children work in mines extracting cobalt that powers the batteries of mobile phones and other electronic devices. The toxic dust of the mines is lost in the dazzle and shimmer of the shops.

It is reported by Amnesty International that children handpick cobalt ore and carry it on their backs as they risk their way out of narrow, collapse-prone, dark tunnels. Whether going into the precarious holes or sifting through rubble, often without protective gear, children get laceration (a deep cut or tear in the skin) and injuries. They inhale harmful dust making them prone to lung disorders. The working hours are long; the breaks are rare.

According to the International LabourOrganisation (ILO), around one million children work in various mines throughout the world. UNICEF (United Nations International Children's Emergency Fund or just the United Nations Children's Fund) estimates that approximately 20% of mine workers are children. They undergo exploitation and are exposed to life threatening chemicals and gases. Children in gold mines get exposed to mercury which is highly toxic.

The ingredient that makes our skin products and nail polishes glister is mica. Mica mines employ children, reportedly, as young as five years old. Horrifyingly, this is because their hands are small enough to fit into the crevices where mica is found.

India is the world's largest producer of mica, which is used in cosmetics and paint production, accounting for 60% of the global production. Mining for the makeup industry's "darkest kept secret" steals the childhood of 20,000 children.

Millions of children are engaged in extreme forms of labour, defined by UN as work which is unacceptable for children. Of this, nearly 70% work in hazardous conditions involving chemicals, pesticides or dangerous machinery. Scores are forced into trafficking, debt bondage and slavery.

Asia-Pacific region harbours the largest number of child workers estimating 127.3 million, while sub Saharan Africa has an estimated 48 million of child workers.

The joint report released by ILO and UNICEF on June 10, 2021 titled "Child Labour: Global Estimates 2020, Trends and the Road Forward" warns that child labour has risen to 160 million (or 16 crore), accounting for almost 1 in 10 children worldwide- an increase of 8.4 million children in the last four years. The report also points out that as economies grapple with COVID-19 and, as a result of it, with increased unemployement and rising poverty, they are exepected to push millions more into child labour.

COVID-19 has had a very bad impact on the economies of countries. More than 23 crore people who were of middle class have now come to below poverty line. Several of the millions of people have lost jobs. A direct effect of all this would be seen on child labour. Children who have not been able to take education in the last two years would be falling out of the education system and would be joining the child labour force.

MNCs behind the scene

It is not only the unorganised sector that uses child labour, as is commonly perceived. Big brands and corporate houses, often known for their lofty ideals and principles, too have a questionable role.

Wal-Mart was fined by the US Department of Labour in 2012 for making children work on dangerous machinery. This fine was believed to be the largest ever levied by the State for child labour. Several leading sportswear brands have been accused of using child labour according to Reuters. It is possible that an expensive pair of shoes brought by you from such brands would be made by a child of about 10-13 years in somewhere in Thailand or Bangladesh after working for approximately 14 hours without any breaks.

Multi-national Companies (MNCs) are making use of hazardous forms of child labour in cotton seed production, according to ILO. Children are hired as their small hands help in cross pollination to produce hybrid seeds. They are exposed to poisonous pesticides in the course of their work.

'The Guardian' reports that about 1.56 million children work under hazardous conditions in cocoa prodction. These children have probably never had the opportunity to taste the chocolates made from their produce.

Several automobile manufacturers, such as Volkwagen and Daimler AG use components coming from units that employ children. Companies claim that it is difficult to verify such information due to the high complexity of automative supply chains, which, is not wrong. If you would read about it, you would understand that their supply chains are actually very complicated and it is quite difficult to verify such information, though not impossible. It, to be done, requires a will. Major tobacco companies have been implicated in child labour, according to WHO.

Companies often exercise a policy of turning a blind eye to these realities. Big MNCs, that so vehemently espouse social responsibility, must know these details. Their supply chains are tainted by child labour. Corporates need to take greater responsibility by refusing to employ children or accepting goods from sub-contractors who do so.

Why Children?

Extreme poverty, illiteracy and ineffective enforcement of laws force children to work. Firms are incentivised to employ children due to low wages. On an average, a child earns 55% less than an adult. Children serve as a readily available pool for labour intensive, low skill jobs.

Employers prefer children due to their submissive behaviour. Children perform out of fear of being abused. Many employers prefer children due to complete absence of labour unrest or disturbances like disputes, protests, strikes, unionisation, etc. In general, the overall contribution of child labour in developing countries is so substantial that stopping it would actually harm the economy and therefore, the issue is often systematically overlooked.

Thus, elimination of child labour requires concerted efforts from government, corporates, NGOs, activists, psychologists and educators. It mandates putting in place concomitant rehabilitation system along with sensitization and education of child workers and their families. Otherwise, child workers who are stopped from working will end up in anti-social acts.

Consumers too have a responsibility. People remain wilfully ignorant because information about ethical attributes of a product can be laden with negative emotions and guilt. Choosing to remain ignorant is a very normal coping mechanism. More diligence is needed to check the abuses of human rights involved in the manufacturing and sourcing of products.

Articles related to Child Labour in the Constitution of India[i]

1. Article 24: Prohibition of employment of children in factories

No child below the age of 14 years shall be employed to work in any factory or mine or engaged in any other hazardous employment. (Fundamental Right)

2. Article 39

(e)The State shall direct its policy towards securing that the health and strength of workers,men and women and the tender age of children are not abused, and that they are not forced by economic necessity to enter vocations unsuitable to their area and strength.

(f) Children shall be given opportunities and facilities to develop in a healthy manner and conditions of freedom and dignity, and that their childhood and youth shall be protected against moral and material abandonment.

3. Article 45

The State shall endeavor to provide within a period of ten years from the commencement of the Constitution, for free and compulsory education for all children until they complete the age of fourteen years. Provision for early childhood care and education to children below the age of six years added by 86th Amendment Act of 2002. (Directive Principle of State Policy)

4. Article 21A: Right to education

Added by 86th Amendment Act, 2002. The State shall provide free and compulsory education to all children of the age of 6 to 14 years in such manner as the State may, by law, determine. (Fundamental Right) Right to education includes right to safe education. (Avinash Mehrotra v. Union of India[ii])

National Legislations addressing the issue of child labour in India

1. The Child Labour (Prohibition and Regulation) Act, 1986[iii]:

(23rd December, 1986)

Based on the recommendations of the Gurupadswammy Committee 1979. It has the following objectives:

(i) To prohibit the engagement of children in certain employment.

(ii) To regulate the conditions of work of children in certain other employments

The act defines a child as any person who has not completed his/her fourteenth year of age.

2. Child Labour (Prohibition and Regulation) Amendment Act, 2016[iv]

(29th July, 2016)

This Act proibited the engagement of children in all occupations and of adolescents in hazardous occupationas and processes. Adolescents refer to those under 18 years and children to those under 14 years of age. It also imposes a fine on anyone who employs or permits children to work.

3. National Policy on Child Labour, 1987

It focuses more on rehabilitation of children working in hazardous occupations and processes, rather than on prevention of child labour.

The policy consists of three main attributes:

(i) Legal Action Plan

Emphasis will be laid on strict and effective enforcement of legal provisions relating to children under various labour laws.

(ii) Focusing on general development programmes

Utilisation of various on-going development programmes of other Ministries/Departments for the benefit of child labour wherever possible.

(iii) Project based plan of action

Launching of projects for the welfare of working children in areas of high concentration of child labour.

Suggestions

1. Government should take proper effective steps to reduce population and give employment to parents of child workers. Control on population growth will reduce poverty which is the basic cause of child labour.

2. Necessary practical steps to be taken to educate the children as enshrined in the Constitution of India.Compulsory education can help in eradicating the problem of child labour to a large extent. Statistics also show that education has helped in reducing child labour in western countries up to a large extent.

3. Provide necessary funds to the organizations working for education of children and removal of child labour like the NGOs as they all have a big role to play in this regard.

4. There should be effective implementation of child protection laws and not overlooked as explained above.

5. Necessary prosecution of child labour defaulters and stricter punishment for those who employ or encourage child labour.

6. Organizing literacy and awareness programmes to prevent children from employment. Awareness raising and mobilization of families and communities against the exploitation of children.

7. Amendment and modification in Social Security Legislation governing child labour.

8. Adequate health services for children at large.

9. Training and education of child workers during their free time.

10. Social protection programmes and cash transfers to improve the economic situation of families so that the need to send children to work is reduced.

11. Every family should earn a decent living and do good saving for the future of its children so that they (the children) can get a decent life and education. It will be very helpful for their children and then people will not need to send their children to work.

12. Each industrial company and organisation should increase the employment opportunities for adult workers and replace child labour with them. Co-ordinated action is required among the government departments to combat the problem of child labour.

According to the InternationLabourOrganisation, there are tremendous benefits for developing nations like India by sending children to school instead of work. But, without education, children do not gain the necessary skills that will increase their productivity to enable them to secure higher skilled jobs in the future with higher wages that will lift them out of poverty. Children who work do not get proper education. Also, their physical, emotional, intellectual and psychological development gets hindered. Therefore, children, who work, instead of going to school, will remain illiterate and this would hinder quality human capital formation.

9 798885 691888

Printed by Libri Plureos GmbH in Hamburg,
Germany